EZRA and NEHEMIAH

A TIME TO REBUILD

12 Studies for Individuals or Groups

JAMES REAPSOME

FISHERMAN

BIBLE STUDYGUIDES

Ezra and Nehemiah
A SHAW BOOK
PUBLISHED BY WATERBROOK PRESS
12265 Oracle Boulevard, Suite 200
Colorado Springs, CO 80921
A division of Random House, Inc.

ISBN 978-0-87788-251-0

Cover photo by Jan Ord

Printed in the United States of America.

CONTENTS

INTRODUCTION

Bible heroes flame across our children's books and Sunday school literature. We see mighty Samson pulling down the temple pillars around him. We see courageous David slaying the giant Goliath. But other heroes like Ezra and Nehemiah draw scant attention. Their stories lie buried in the old records that we tend to skip. After all, what's so exciting about rebuilding a burned-out city and temple?

But when we prick the surface we discover high drama in the lives of both Ezra and Nehemiah. Called by God to restore Jerusalem's walls and worship, these men confronted powerful enemies outside their camp and grievous sins within the family. Their stories follow the Bible's major theme—that great faith demands great courage and unusual obedience to God.

Their stories make compelling reading because Ezra and Nehemiah enter the biblical saga of the Jews at a critical juncture of the survival of the nation politically and spiritually. Having endured seventy years in Babylon, the Jews were ready to go back to their homes, their temple, and their faith. But great movements require great leaders. God called Ezra and Nehemiah and they complied, but not without great risks.

Ezra, the doctor of the law, and Nehemiah, the doctor of engineering, both were needed to fulfill God's plan to redeem and restore his people. From their vision, prayers, wisdom, courage, and faith we can draw remarkable applications to Christian living. They show us what legitimate, powerful spiritual leadership is all about.

Travel the pages of dramatic history with them. You will find yourself enthralled with what Ezra and Nehemiah accomplished under the good hand of the Lord.

HOW TO USE THIS STUDYGUIDE

Fisherman studyguides are based on the inductive approach to Bible study. Inductive study is discovery study; we discover what the Bible says as we ask questions about its content and search for answers. This is quite different from the process in which a teacher *tells* a group *about* the Bible, what it means, and what to do about it. In inductive study, God speaks directly to each of us through his Word.

A group functions best when a leader keeps the discussion on target, but this leader is neither the teacher nor the "answer person." A leader's responsibility is to *ask*—not *tell*. The answers come from the text itself as group members examine, discuss, and think together about the passage.

There are four kinds of questions in each study. The first is an *approach question.* Used before the Bible passage is read, this question breaks the ice and helps you focus on the topic of the Bible study. It begins to reveal where thoughts and feelings need to be transformed by Scripture.

Some of the earlier questions in each study are *observation question* designed to help you find out basic facts—who, what, where, when, and how.

When you know what the Bible says, you need to ask, *What does it mean?* These *interpretation questions* help you to discover the writer's basic message.

Application questions ask, *What does it mean to me?* They challenge you to live out the Scripture's life-transforming message.

Fisherman studyguides provide spaces between questions for jotting down responses and related questions you would like to raise in the group. Each group member should have a copy of the studyguide and may take a turn in leading the group.

For consistency, Fisherman guides are written from the *New International Version.* But a group should feel free to use the NIV or any other accurate, modern translation of the Bible such as the *New Living Translation,* the *New Revised Standard Version,* the *New Jerusalem Bible,* or the *Good News Bible.* (Paraphrases of the Bible may be referred to when additional help is needed.) Bible commentaries should not be brought to a Bible study because they tend to dampen discussion and keep people from thinking for themselves.

SUGGESTIONS FOR GROUP LEADERS

1. Read and study the Bible passage thoroughly beforehand, grasping its themes and applying its teachings for yourself. Pray that the Holy Spirit will "guide you into truth" so that your leadership will guide others.

2. If the studyguide's questions ever seem ambiguous or unnatural to you, rephrase them, feeling free to add others that seem necessary to bring out the meaning of a verse.

3. Begin (and end) the study promptly. Start by asking someone to pray for God's help. Remember, the Holy Spirit is the teacher, not you!

4. Ask for volunteers to read the passages out loud.

5. As you ask the studyguide's questions in sequence, encourage everyone to participate in the discussion. If some are silent, ask, "What do you think, Heather?" or "Dan, what can you add to that answer?" or suggest, "Let's have an answer from someone who hasn't spoken up yet."

6. If a question comes up that you can't answer, don't be afraid to admit that you're baffled! Assign the topic as a research project for someone to report on next week.

7. Keep the discussion moving and focused. Though tangents will inevitably be introduced, you can bring the discussion back to the topic at hand. Learn to pace the discussion so that you finish a study each session you meet.

8. Don't be afraid of silences; some questions take time to answer and some people need time to gather courage to speak. If silence persists, rephrase your question, but resist the temptation to answer it yourself.

9. If someone comes up with an answer that is clearly illogical or unbiblical, ask him or her for further clarification: "What verse suggests that to you?"

10. Discourage Bible-hopping and overuse of cross-references. Learn all you can from *this* passage, along with a few important references suggested in the studyguide.

11. Some questions are marked with a ◆. This indicates that further information is available in the Leader's Notes at the back of the guide.

12. For further information on getting a new Bible study group started and keeping it functioning effectively, read Gladys Hunt's *You Can Start a Bible Study Group* and *Pilgrims in Progress: Growing through Groups* by Jim and Carol Plueddemann.

SUGGESTIONS FOR GROUP MEMBERS

1. Learn and apply the following ground rules for effective Bible study. (If new members join the group later, review these guidelines with the whole group.)

2. Remember that your goal is to learn all that you can *from the Bible passage being studied.* Let it speak for itself without using Bible commentaries or other Bible passages. There is more than enough in each assigned passage to keep your group productively occupied for one session. Sticking to the passage saves the group from insecurity and confusion.

3. Avoid the temptation to bring up those fascinating tangents that don't really grow out of the passage you are discussing. If the topic is of common interest, you can bring it up later in informal conversation following the study. Meanwhile, help each other stick to the subject!

4. Encourage each other to participate. People remember best what they discover and verbalize for themselves. Some people are naturally shier than others, or they may be afraid of making a mistake. If your discussion is free and friendly and you show real interest in what other group members think and feel, they will be more likely to speak up. Remember, the more people involved in a discussion, the richer it will be.

5. Guard yourself from answering too many questions or talking too much. Give others a chance to express themselves. If you are one who participates easily, discipline yourself by counting to ten before you open your mouth!

6. Make personal, honest applications and commit yourself to letting God's Word change you.

GOING HOME!

Ezra 1–2

During World War II in Europe millions of Jews suffered death, imprisonment, and deportation. They were forced from their homes in cities, towns, and villages. Long afterwards, a church in one city in Austria decided to invite the Jews who had been expelled to come back and visit their home city—with all expenses paid by the Christians. At first the Jews were reticent to accept, but they did come, and they shared an emotional homecoming that satisfied their long pent-up desires.

This is something of what it must have been like when the Jewish exiles in Babylon heard about the decree of Cyrus allowing them to go back to Jerusalem. Ezra's story begins with this totally unexpected proclamation. In this study we learn the background of what Ezra was later called on to do for God and his people.

1. When have you experienced God's unexpected intervention in your life when you had given up hope?

Read Ezra 1.

◆ **2.** Who moved Cyrus to act?

To whom did Cyrus give credit for his empire?

◆ **3.** What do these facts tell us about political developments in our time? How should we pray?

4. Identify the main points of Cyrus's decree (verses 2-4).

How did he refer to God? Why?

5. What was the purpose of the collection (verse 4)?

Who was to provide the resources?

◆ **6.** Note who took action after Cyrus's proclamation (verse 5). What was their mission?

◆ **7.** How do you think God had moved their hearts?

How does he do that today in our lives?

8. How did the Jews' neighbors respond to Cyrus's decree (verse 6)?

How would you have felt if you were a local Babylonian and had to give things to the departing captives?

9. Why do you think Cyrus contributed so much (verses 7-11)?

How would this act have affected you as a Jew?

Read Ezra 2.

◆ **10.** What was the point of naming the families of the exiles who returned to Jerusalem?

◆ **11.** How had the worship of God been preserved among those who returned (verses 36, 40-43)?

12. Consider the offerings given to rebuild the temple (verses 68-69). It amounted to 1,100 pounds of gold and 3 tons of silver. How do you account for their wealth and their generosity?

13. What contributions can you make to further God's work in your community and around the world?

REBUILDING AMIDST OBSTACLES

Ezra 3–4

Despite their fears amid their enemies, the Jewish exiles' first act was to worship God when they returned to Jerusalem. Then they tackled the difficult work of rebuilding their temple. This incited serious opposition, and eventually their work ceased because of the king's edict. When we are serious about our spiritual growth, we must count the costs. If our worship and our work are to please God, we must overcome our fears and other obstacles.

1. How do you react when facing opposition to something you want to do?

Read Ezra 3.

2. After they had settled, what was the first order of business for the Jews (verses 1-6)?

3. What could have hindered them from doing this (verse 3)?

Why do you think they went ahead anyway?

◆ **4.** When have you had to overcome fears of people around you in order to obey the Lord?

◆ **5.** How was the next order of business organized and accomplished (verses 7-9)?

6. When the foundation was laid, what was the theme of their celebration (verse 11)?

◆ **7.** How could they say, "God is good and he loves Israel," after what they had endured in judgment and captivity?

8. Among the people, what responses marked their celebration (verses 11-13)? What made the difference?

In what circumstances are we sometimes happy and sad at the same time? Why?

Read Ezra 4.

9. What did the enemies of the Jews offer to do (verses 1-2)? Why?

◆ **10.** Why did the leaders of Israel respond as they did (verse 3)?

How do we know when it is right or wrong to accept help from unbelievers? What issues are at stake?

◆ **11.** Put the gist of the correspondence to and from King Artaxerxes in your own words (verses 11-23). What were the main accusations they brought up?

12. What modern-day or personal examples can you think of that compare to this opposition to and halting of the work of the Lord?

◆ **13.** What is our responsibility when enemies seek to stop the advance of the gospel and the church?

THE TEMPLE DEDICATED

Ezra 5–6

During occasional road trips my wife and I often passed what looked like the start of a new church building. We saw the foundation walls and the flooring built and expected to see continuing work. Yet, over a decade all that was added was tar paper to cover the first floor. Apparently the basement was the only thing completed before the project had ground to a halt.

Jerusalem's temple project also proceeded by fits and starts. In their struggle to make a new life for themselves, the Jews neglected to finish the temple. Their enemies discouraged them and they finally resorted to paperwork—the equivalent of trying to get a building permit from city hall after you have already begun building. God not only took care of the paperwork, he also recharged the people by sending them forceful prophets to spur them on to finish.

1. What things has God used in your life to give you a fresh start or to help you complete what looked like an impossible task?

Read Ezra 5.

◆ **2.** Who urged the people to start building again (verses 1-2)?

What do you imagine they said?

3. How would the prophets' presence have affected the people (verse 2)?

◆ **4.** What are ways we can encourage and strengthen one another to do God's will?

5. What new problem developed (verses 3-5)?

How did the Jews respond?

◆ **6.** Summarize the main points of the letter from the officials to King Darius (verses 8-17).

◆ **7.** What line of argument did the Jews give in defense of their work (verses 11-15)?

What does this tell us about their understanding of past events in their history?

◆ **8.** Why is it important to keep a record of our spiritual journeys with the Lord?

Read Ezra 6.

◆ **9.** Having found the decree of King Cyrus (verses 1-5), what commands did Darius give the governor to help the Jews (verses 6-12)?

Why do you think he asked for prayer (verse 10)?

10. How do you explain the king's attitude toward the Jewish temple and toward God?

11. Imagine the roles of Haggai and Zechariah in completing the work (5:1-2; 6:13-15).

Why do we need constant encouragement from the Lord?

◆ **12.** The Jews celebrated the dedication of the temple (verses 16-18), and then they kept the Passover and the Feast of Unleavened Bread (verses 19-22). How does participation in the church's celebrations reflect what God has done for us and help us spiritually?

GOD'S LEADER ARRIVES

Ezra 7

Choosing leaders for God's work in our churches is not an easy task. For one thing, we tend to equate outward qualities with spiritual leadership. People who are outgoing, easy talkers, educated, good-looking, wealthy, and leaders in their professions tend to be among our first choices. But God has different criteria.

Ezra's story shows that when God needed a leader to renew Jerusalem's spiritual vitality, he chose an obscure priest and teacher who was faithfully performing his behind-the-scenes duties—not for public acclaim but for God's approval. He was another example of God's selection process: looking not at the outward appearance but at the heart (1 Samuel 16:7).

1. Recall your latest choice for church leaders. How did you choose them?

◆ Read Ezra 7.

◆ **2.** What was Ezra's occupation? What were his qualifications (verses 6, 10-11)?

◆ **3.** How did Ezra explain the king's grant and his safe journey from Babylon to Jerusalem (verses 6, 9)?

When have you experienced "the gracious hand of God" intervening for your good?

4. Describe the main points of the king's assignment to Ezra before he left Bablyon (verses 11-20).

◆ **5.** Why were the sacrifices on the altar important?

What kinds of sacrifices does God call on us to make today?

6. What were the king's treasurers to do and not do (verses 21-24)?

7. Why do you think Artaxerxes was concerned about the worship of God?

8. What further assignment did the king give to Ezra (verses 25-26)? Why?

◆ **9.** In what ways can our government and society be taught the laws of God?

What roles do churches and Christian families play?

10. How did Ezra react to the king's letter (verses 27-28)?

To whom did he give credit?

11. For what daily "commissions"—small or large—do you need special courage from the Lord?

◆ **12.** Why do you think God chose a person like Ezra to head this mission back to Jerusalem?

13. What can we learn from this story about what qualities to look for in spiritual leaders today?

THE JOURNEY COMPLETED

Ezra 8

Stories of Christian missionary pioneers reveal that many times they had to make quick decisions in times of danger. They often lacked the kind of safeguards we take for granted today. As they forged into unknown territories, they had to decide how to cross rivers, fend off wild animals, and make peace with the villagers. They counted on their friends at home to pray for their protection. Many times their own prayers were instantaneous. We might consider some of them foolhardy daredevils who took unnecessary risks, but they thrived on courage and faith.

Ezra faced similar challenges when he contemplated his journey from Babylon to Jerusalem. He was facing new territory—the responsibility for a huge assembly of people. Strong faith was required. His story reminds us of the unusual qualities demanded of leaders.

1. Some Christians argue that we needn't bother God with the details of our lives. Others pray meticulously about everything. How do faith and courage and prayer blend in your Christian experience?

Read Ezra 8.

◆ **2.** The returning exiles were classified by families, probably totaling around 3,000 people. What problem confronted Ezra when he left Babylon (verse 15)?

Why was this important?

3. Who was brought to Ezra as a solution (verses 16-20)?

◆ **4.** Why did Ezra proclaim a fast (verses 21-22)?

5. Why do you think he was ashamed and told the king that he did not need protection before he fasted and prayed?

As a leader, was this foolish, presumptuous, or a sign of faith?

6. Under what circumstances might we be called upon to make a strong declaration of our faith in God before we have had a chance to pray about it?

◆ **7.** What is the place of fasting and prayer in Christian life today?

8. The journey to Jerusalem had not yet begun. What further matters concerned Ezra (verses 24-30)?

What did the offerings and the temple articles represent?

9. They faced many dangers on their journey. How did they make it to Jerusalem without the king's soldiers (verses 31-32)?

10. Imagine the scene in Jerusalem when Ezra and his group arrive. Give a word picture of what happened (verses 33-36). What spirit of the day would you like to capture in your picture?

11. What effect did the king's orders have (verse 36)?

◆ **12.** How would you rate Ezra as a leader thus far? Why?

Which of his qualities would you like to have?

SIN PURGED

Ezra 9–10

The executive committee of a Christian organization gathered to hear their director's report. He stunned them by announcing that he was resigning because of marital infidelity. Joyful expectations were plunged into deep gloom, hurt, and anger as the committee accepted the man's resignation.

Sin in the ranks of God's people is nothing new. Following the arduous journey back to Jerusalem, the returning exiles were enjoying renewed worship and hope. But Ezra's joyous celebration and expectations turned sour when sin was discovered among God's people. Ezra dealt with the issues head-on, taking some highly unusual steps for a leader to take.

1. Why are private and public confessions of our sins so critical in the development of a strong Christian faith and community?

Read Ezra 9.

◆ **2.** The interval between the events of chapters 8 and 9 was probably four months. What problem did the leaders bring to Ezra's attention now (verses 1-2)?

◆ **3.** How do you explain Ezra's dramatic reaction (verses 3-5)?

◆ **4.** Review Ezra's prayer in verses 6-15 and summarize the main points.

Opening of prayer (verses 6-7):

Praise for what God had done (verses 8-9):

Sins confessed (verses 10-15):

5. To what attributes of God did he appeal (verses 13-15)? Why?

6. Imagine you were one of those gathered with Ezra and heard his prayer. How do you think you would have felt? Why?

◆ **7.** Think about the components of Ezra's prayer. How can his prayer be a model for our prayer lives, public and private?

Read Ezra 10:1-17.

◆ **8.** How were the people affected by Ezra's confession (verses 1-4)?

9. What do Ezra's actions in verses 5-6 tell us about his walk with God and his understanding of sin?

10. Ezra reiterated the charges and the consequences. How was his sermon received (verses 12-15)? Why?

◆ **11.** Skim verses 18-44. What do you think was the point of naming names?

12. What do you think this public confession and the separation from foreign wives accomplished in Israel?

◆ **13.** As we close this study on Ezra, reflect on his life and work.

What kind of a person was Ezra?

What did he do for his people?

Would you have followed his leadership? Why?

NEHEMIAH'S MISSION LAUNCHED

Nehemiah 1–2

Crowds gather at Cape Canaveral, Florida, to watch the awesome display of power whenever NASA schedules a new space launch. Something about the earth-rattling effects of mighty rocket blastoffs leaves us momentarily transfixed.

The launching of Nehemiah's mission to rebuild Jerusalem was akin to a rocket blastoff. Against all odds, this humble servant of the mighty Persian emperor was given permission to return to the devastated homeland of the conquered Jews. Defying all political and religious laws of gravity, he not only got the green light but also got the papers, the building materials, and the Persian cavalry to accompany him. He launched his mission not with millions of pounds of jet thrust, but with the hand of Almighty God.

1. Think about a difficult situation—either in your own life or in the lives of some of your friends—where serious help and "repairs" are needed. What encourages you to intervene? To not intervene? How do you decide?

◆ **Read Nehemiah 1.**

◆ **2.** What was Nehemiah's occupation and where did he serve (verses 1, 11)?

◆ **3.** How did he react to the news about conditions in Jerusalem (verses 2-4)? Why?

4. In what three ways did he reveal the condition of his soul (verse 4)?

◆ **5.** Analyze Nehemiah's prayer (verses 5-11).

What elements of praise and worship do you find?

What elements of confession?

What promise of God?

What elements of petition?

Read Nehemiah 2:1-10.

6. What startling request did Nehemiah make of the king (verses 1-5)?

How do you account for his clarity and boldness?

◆ **7.** What specific things did he ask the king to provide, and what did the king offer (verses 6-8)?

8. Four months had passed between Nehemiah's prayer and his opportunity to importune the king. How do his responses to the king reveal what he had been thinking and praying about during that time?

What are the keys to successful strikes for God when he suddenly opens the doors?

Read Nehemiah 2:11-20.

◆ **9.** Summarize what Nehemiah found when he returned to Jerusalem (verses 11-15).

◆ **10.** In the drama about to unfold, what two groups will be the protagonists (verses 10, 16-19)?

What were their initial responses to Nehemiah's courageous proposal? Why?

11. Why was Nehemiah so certain of success (verses 8b, 12, 18, 20)?

What was Nehemiah's part in his mission? God's part?

12. How does the successful launch of his mission serve to build your faith in God?

PERSISTING DESPITE OPPOSITION

Nehemiah 3–5

Roadblocks to Christian faith and obedience were promised by Jesus and the apostles. Jesus warned that his students would be hailed before the courts, and people who killed them would think they were doing God a favor. Nehemiah's cause was likewise hindered by ridicule and death threats. In addition, his own people prejudiced his cause and dishonored God by their sinful dealings with their fellow Jews.

Nehemiah's story helps us to grasp the principles of faith at work—prayer, vigilance, courage, and hard work. This dramatic episode also reveals what Nehemiah was made of and why he was God's man to lead the rebuilding of Jerusalem.

1. What hindrances to faith and obedience to God have you faced recently in your life?

Read Nehemiah 3.

2. Having rejected the mockery of their enemies and professing their faith in God, the Jews set about rebuilding Jerusalem's walls. How did they accomplish their tasks?

Why do you think they set about it in such a precise, well-organized way?

◆ 3. Consider the wide range of vocations represented in this hard manual labor. What does this reveal about Nehemiah as a motivator and leader?

What strengths and gifts did he bring to his vision?

◆ 4. Willingness to work and a spirit of cooperation are essential to the successful completion of any project. Talk about some projects to advance God's kingdom you might want to join. What will be required of you? Of your friends?

Read Nehemiah 4.

◆ **5.** How might the ridicule and mockery of Sanballat and Tobiah have affected the Jews working on the gates and walls (verses 1-3)?

◆ **6.** Why was it important to pray at this juncture (verses 4-5)?

Who do you think said the prayer? Who do you think heard it?

7. Ridicule and mockery failed to stop the work (verse 6). What strategies did Sanballat, Tobiah, and their cohorts come up with next (verses 8-12)?

◆ **8.** Discuss the major elements in Nehemiah's strategy to overcome these obstacles (verses 9, 13-14). How did he meld the practical and the spiritual aspects, or, as we might say, how did "works and faith" work together?

9. To whom did the Jews attribute their desire to return to work (verse 15)?

How does our knowledge of God's character build our faith and hard work?

◆ **10.** How did the plans devised by Nehemiah give them the courage and energy to keep going (verses 16-23)?

Read Nehemiah 5.

◆ **11.** New troubles arose from within the city. What was the essential nature of the complaints among the Jews themselves (verses 1-5)?

◆ **12.** What was the outcome of Nehemiah's angry accusations (verses 6-13)?

What more did Nehemiah do (verses 14-19)?

13. How did this episode bring out additional qualities of leadership in Nehemiah?

In what situations can you implement the high principles of righteous living this week?

REACHING THE GOAL

Nehemiah 6–7

The joys of a day at the beach are not unalloyed. Besides risk-ing sunburn, we spend too much time swatting at pesky flies. They love to bite our legs, and we can't hit all of them. Nehemiah's building project was likewise hindered because those pagan "flies"—Sanballat and Tobiah—would not leave him alone. They bit him here and they bit him there, but he refused to quit. With renewed determination, hard work, clear thinking, and prayer, he and the Israelites persisted and the wall was completed in fifty-two days.

1. Think about a time when you did not complete or finish a project. What things kept you from reaching the goal?

Read Nehemiah 6.

◆ **2.** Having divided his team between builders and guards, Nehemiah vigorously pursued the rebuilding of Jerusalem's gates and walls (4:16-23). What response did this draw from their enemies (6:1-2)?

◆ **3.** Why did Nehemiah refuse to listen to their offer of peace talks (verses 3-4)?

In what way was their persistence a test of his faith and courage?

◆ **4.** What biblical principles serve as guidelines for us when we are tempted to make deals with the enemy?

◆ **5.** How did Sanballet turn up the screws on Nehemiah (verses 5-7)?

What was behind his scheme (verse 9)?

6. Analyze the two parts of Nehemiah's defense (verses 8-9). How do they illustrate the governing principle of his life—using his brains (work) and his faith?

Reflect on New Testament illustrations of this truth: Ephesians 2:8-10; 6:13; Philippians 4:13-14; Colossians 1:28-29. What do you find?

◆ **7.** Having thus failed to entice Nehemiah into a trap, what clever subversion did Sanballet and Tobiah try next (verses 10-13; 17-19)?

◆ **8.** What was the big issue at stake in this incident (verse 13)?

Why was this crucial to the success of Nehemiah's mission?

9. When Nehemiah asked God to "remember" his enemies, what do you think he had in mind (verse 14)?

Why was such a prayer justified?

10. What did the completion of the wall in fifty-two days say to the surrounding pagans (verses 15-16)?

Read Nehemiah 7.

◆ **11.** What was behind Nehemiah's strategy for the gates (verses 1-3)?

Why was this necessary?

◆ **12.** Of what value were the genealogy and the other records (verses 4-73)?

13. Highlight the significant elements of this startling accomplishment of rebuilding the wall. What do they mean to you in your Christian growth?

GOD'S LAW REDISCOVERED

Nehemiah 8–9

The Israelites have completed the new wall around Jerusalem and have settled in to their homeland. This study begins with a glorious celebration in Jerusalem where God's Word was honored and taught. But just as medical tests often reveal signs of cancer or disease, so God's Law revealed a history of spiritual cancer in the Israelites' long history. Let's see what repercussions the reading of God's Word had on people.

1. When has a verse or passage of the Bible convicted you of sin or encouraged you in a specific way? Explain.

Read Nehemiah 8.

◆ **2.** Pretend you are the director of a Hollywood production of this scene. What characters and elements would you want to emphasize?

What emotional impact would you want to convey?

◆ **3.** Why do you think the people had such great respect for the Law?

4. In your life what circumstances create a hunger for God's Word?

5. What was the major thrust of Nehemiah's instruction (verse 10)?

◆ **6.** Why was celebration in order?

What occasions call for great Christian celebrations? Why?

7. What qualities of leadership did Nehemiah display on this occasion?

Read Nehemiah 9.

8. Three weeks later the Jews gathered again, not to celebrate, but to confess their sins and worship the Lord. How do you account for this somber occasion, in light of the facts of chapter 8? (See 8:9-11).

◆ **9.** What elements of God's character did the Levites cite again and again?

How do you think they had attained such an amazing grasp of Israel's history?

10. Summarize what God had done for his people. How had they responded to him?

What was the essence of their failures?

11. How did the Levites describe the present condition of the Jews (verses 36-37)?

◆ **12.** What was the purpose of their confession (verses 3, 38; see also 10:28)?

Why is the acknowledgment of our sins so important?

◆ **13.** How would you trace the history of God's dealings with you, starting with the gospel story?

COVENANT CONFIRMED

Nehemiah 10–12

We all make covenants of one kind or another. By signing legal documents, we agree to fulfill the terms of the contract. When we stand before our friends to declare our love and loyalty to our spouses-to-be, we make serious vows and commitments. When we become a member of a church, we make a promise to be an active part of that body. But the greatest promise of all is our promise to be faithful to Christ.

Ezra and Nehemiah led the people in confession and then helped them make a new covenant with the Lord. They took steps to bring the people to Jerusalem as permanent inhabitants. They also recognized the critical importance of establishing worship according to God's laws. Theirs was not a pick-and-choose religion. The people not only found new homes, they also found a new spirit of praise and worship.

1. What commitments or vows are most important to you?

Read Nehemiah 10.

2. This is the text of the binding agreement (or covenant) the people made with God after confessing their sins (9:38). Who was the first to sign it?

What example did Nehemiah, the Levites, and the leaders set for the rest of the people?

3. Describe their commitments to action in each major section of their agreement:

Verses 28-29:

Verse 30:

Verse 31:

Verses 32-33:

Verses 34-35:

Verses 36-39:

◆ **4.** What were the most pervasive themes of their promises?

How would you describe the effect of these promises on everyday life and worship in Jerusalem?

◆ **5.** What promises do we make when we make a faith commitment to Jesus Christ as our Lord and Savior?

Why are we often so leery of making financial commitments to Christ and his church, as the Israelites did for their temple worship?

Skim Nehemiah 11.

Chapters 8–10 focused on spiritual renewal in Jerusalem under Ezra's leadership. In chapter 11, the story of the rebuilding and resettlement of Jerusalem picks up from Nehemiah 7:4. The city was largely uninhabited, except for the city's leaders. To populate the city, they held a lottery and then others came voluntarily (11:1).

Skim Nehemiah 12:1-26.

In verses 1-7 we find the list of the priests who, 93 years before, had returned to Jerusalem from Babylon with Zerubbabel and Jeshua, and in verses 8-9, the names of the Levites. The list of priests (verses 12-21) is from the high priesthood of Jeshua's son Joiakim. The names of the gatekeepers (verses 25-26) are from the days of Joiakim and the days of Nehemiah and Ezra,

Read Nehemiah 12:27-47.

6. What groups were organized for the dedication of the wall of Jerusalem (verses 27-30)?

7. What was the theme of the celebration (verse 27)?

◆ **8.** What was required of the spiritual leaders, the people, the gates, and the wall (verse 30)? Why?

◆ **9.** Why must we be pure to worship the Lord?

How are we purified to do so?

10. How did the ministry of the two choirs contribute to the dedication (verses 31-43)?

What was the theme of their music (verses 31, 40)?

11. Why was it important to put people in charge of the offerings (verse 44)?

◆ **12.** What great record of faithfulness was achieved by the people under Nehemiah's leadership (verses 45-47)?

Why was it important to celebrate this fact?

LIVING UP TO THE CALL

Nehemiah 13

In Geneva, Switzerland, there is a remarkable memorial called the Wall of the Reformers. There we see the bigger-than-life likenesses of John Calvin, John Knox, Theodore de Beze, and Guillaume Farel. They obeyed God's call to reestablish the fundamentals of Christian faith and doctrine.

Nehemiah was a person like that. We have seen his remarkable courage and faith, his intelligent planning and building, his morale-boosting leadership, and his prayers. In this closing chapter we see a leader determined to root out seemingly incidental shortcomings among the country's religious leaders as well as the people. Very simply, Nehemiah brooked not even the slightest deviation from God's holy laws, because he knew the nation's welfare depended on obedience.

1. What reforms in our nation's history have most inspired you? Why?

◆ Read Nehemiah 13.

◆ **2.** As you look over this chaptcr, how did Nehemiah uphold the laws of God?

Why was he such a stickler for 100 percent compliance?

3. What overall sense of Nehemiah's character, godliness, and leadership do you get from his reforms?

What were his strengths? His weaknesses?

◆ **4.** Why do you think he treated his foes and the law-breakers so roughly (verses 7-11, 17-18, 21, 25)?

Was this necessary?

5. Identify each category of leaders Nehemiah addressed (verses 4-8, 11, 17, 20, 28).

Why didn't he try to work out some compromises with these people?

6. In what situations have you been called to stand up for righteousness? Why?

7. What view of God did Nehemiah have?

What difference did this make in his actions?

8. How does your understanding of who God is affect your attitudes and conduct?

9. Note his short prayers in verses 14, 22b, 29, and 31b. What was his major prayer concern at this time in his life? Why?

10. God uses many different people to influence us for good. Who have been the spiritual-change agents in your life?

In whose lives can you be someone like Nehemiah was?

11. Review Nehemiah's prayers: 1:5-11; 4:4-5; 5:19; 6:9, 14; 13:14, 22, 29, 31b. What is most impressive about his prayers? Why?

12. Review chapter 5 and put it with Nehemiah's reforms in chapter 13. Considering that he came to Jerusalem to rebuild its gates and walls, what do you think were his major accomplishments? Why?

13. Pray and thank God for Ezra and Nehemiah's commitment and leadership. Ask him to help you be the kind of leader he wants you to be in your family, among your circle of friends and coworkers, in your church, and in your community.

LEADER'S NOTES

Study 1/Going Home!

Question 2. As the book of Ezra opens, we find God's people exiled in foreign Babylon. Jeremiah had prophesied that the captivity of the Jews in Babylon would end after seventy years (Jeremiah 25:12; 29:10). Isaiah had prophesied that God would use Cyrus to accomplish this (Isaiah 44:28–45:1). Jeremiah 52 describes the downfall of Jerusalem and the deportation of the Jews to Babylon. Your group may want to reflect on the condition of the Jews in Babylon as seen in Psalm 137:1-6 and Nehemiah 1:4.

Cyrus overthrew the Babylonian Empire in 539 B.C. The record in Ezra follows that of 2 Chronicles 36:22-23. Ezra 1–2 describes the return of the first group of exiles. The temple had been rebuilt and dedicated in 515 B.C. (chapters 3–6). Ezra himself did not return to Jerusalem until some eighty years later in 458 B.C. (chapters 7–10).

Question 3. Keep the big picture in mind. It would not be appropriate to try to predict the future or to say with absolute certainty which political views are necessarily in line with

God's will. But we know that God is ultimately in control of events of history.

Question 6. The tribes of Judah and Benjamin were the survivors of the original twelve tribes of Israel. The other ten tribes had been carried off by the Assyrians in 722 B.C. and through intermarriage had lost their identity. For the destruction wrought by Nebuchadnezzar, see 2 Chronicles 36:17-20 and Jeremiah 51:34.

Question 7. Do not let your group fall into vague generalities in answering how God moves in people's hearts today. Ask for specific examples that will be helpful to others. Be prepared with some of your own.

Question 10. The total number of those returning came to almost 50,000. Many Jews remained in Babylon because they did not want to abandon their thriving businesses. The leaders mentioned included Zerubbabel (Ezra 2:2), but not Sheshbazzar (Ezra 1:8). It is not known, but perhaps Sheshbazzar died soon after returning to Jerusalem and Zerubbabel took his place. The Nehemiah named here is not the man who arrived in Jerusalem ninety-two years later.

Question 11. It was important to reestablish the roles of the priests, Levites, singers, and gatekeepers. They had preserved the ancient rituals surrounding the true worship of God. Family geneology was important here (Ezra 2:59, 62-63). Those who could not prove their ancestry were barred from the priesthood. Urim and Thummin (verse 63) were sacred stones used to determine God's will in certain matters.

Study 2/Rebuilding Amidst Obstacles

Question 4. Take time to discuss two or three specific examples of how fear inhibits our witness to Christ and our obedience to God's moral laws.

Question 5. The people from Sidon and Tyre were Phoenicians. Compare this temple construction with that of Solomon's temple (2 Chronicles 2:1-16).

Question 7. This is a tough issue to discuss. It reflects our need to be fully convinced about God's character and the purposes of His work in our lives through Christ. See Romans 8:28-39.

Question 10. The enemies here were the mixed people later known as the Samaritans. They professed to worship God, but they also worshiped idols (2 Kings 17:24-41). So in this context, the risks of idolatry were high. The Jews knew God's judgment for their own idolatry. Be prepared to discuss differences on this subject. The New Testament principle is found in 2 Corinthians 6:14-18.

Question 11. Note that Ezra 4:1-5 describes opposition to rebuilding the temple, while Ezra 4:6-23 refers to rebuilding the walls of Jerusalem (verses 12, 16). The setting of Ezra 4:1-5 is during the reigns of Cyrus and Cambyses (not mentioned in Ezra or Nehemiah) and the beginning of the reign of Darius I (538–520 B.C.). Ezra 4:6-23 reflects the reign of Artaxerxes (464–424 B.C.).

The work came to a standstill for fifteen years. Ezra 4:6-23 interrupts the chronological sequence of the story to carry the account of the opposition through to the time of Ezra and Nehemiah. Aramaic (4:7) was the international diplomatic language of the Persian Empire.

Question 13. Allow time for thoughtful reflection. Encourage simple, practical answers.

Study 3/The Temple Dedicated

Question 2. We find in the book of Haggai that stoppage of the work on the temple was caused not only by the enemies of the Jews to their north but also by the Jews giving priority to building big houses for themselves. Consequently, the Lord had sent drought and famine (see Haggai 1). God sent these prophets to Judah and Jerusalem after the exile in Babylon had ended. Spiritually and economically, the people were impoverished at this time. Haggai and Zechariah addressed the low levels of spiritual life. Rebuilding of the temple began within a month of Haggai's first sermon, and it was completed four years after Haggai predicted it would be done. (Read Haggai and Zechariah 1–8 for further insights into conditions in Jerusalem and their ministries at this time.)

Question 4. Look for examples of specific things we can do for one another. This ministry is not limited to the roles of pastors.

Question 6. The letter to King Darius sought to find out if the Jews had obtained the proper permissions for their work. Here we find ancient bureaucracy at work. This was not a case of official hostility and opposition. However, the leader of the Jews, Zerubbabel, was terrified because he thought the inquiry would halt the work for good. Zechariah told him that God's Spirit would prevail and the temple would be completed (Zechariah 4:6-9).

For historical context, these are the Persian kings who ruled during the days of Ezra, Nehemiah, Haggai, Zechariah, and Malachi: Cyrus (559–530 B.C.), Cambyses (530–522), Darius I (522–486), Xerxes I (486–465), Artaxerxes I (464–423). See Ezra 4:5, 24; 5 for Darius I; Ezra 4:6 for Xerxes I (also called Ahasuerus); Ezra 4:7-23; 7:1-26 for Artaxerxes I.

Question 7. The great king of Israel (verse 11) was King Solomon. Note how the governor contrasted the behavior of the Babylonians (Nebuchadnezzar) and the Persians (Cyrus) in verses 12-14.

Question 8. Journaling is a helpful practice for many people. Whether or not we keep journals is not the main point here. However we do it, we must find a discipline to help us recall and transmit from one generation to the next the distinctive milestones of God's grace in our lives.

Question 9. The decree of Cyrus could not be found at Babylon, but it was found at Ecbatana, the capital of Media and the summer home of the Persian kings. Darius added to the original decree by requiring the provision of all the money and supplies the Jews would need. The original obstruction planned by the enemies of the Jews thus backfired.

Question 12. The temple dedication followed the pattern set by King Solomon (1 Kings 8:63). The Passover was celebrated on the date commanded at its institution (Exodus 12:18). Passover commemorated God's deliverance of the Jews when the death angel struck Egypt. The Feast of Unleavened Bread was commanded in Leviticus 23:6. Check your Bible dictionary for further details about these observances, but do not spend too much time discussing them.

Make this question a time of personal reflection, not just a critique of what various churches do. Talk about how individual participation in the sacraments or church celebrations can enhance spiritual growth and development.

Study 4/God's Leader Arrives

General background. The book of Ezra gets its name from Ezra's personal memoirs in chapters 7–10. Chronologically, this section follows Nehemiah 1–7; Ezra's memoirs continue in Nehemiah 8–10. The events of Ezra 7 are dated by the reign of King Artaxerxes I, which means a period of fifty-eight years after the events of chapter 6. During this time the accusations against the Jews occurred (Ezra 4:6), the events described in the book of Esther took place, and Malachi was the prophet.

Question 2. In contemporary terms, Ezra was a doctor of the law. His ancestry (Ezra 7:1-5) was important because it validated the authority he needed to carry out his mission.

Question 3. See also Ezra 8:18, 22, 31. Part of God's provision was Ezra's close personal contact with the king. He probably was the Jews' representative at the court. The king called him "a teacher of the Law of the God of heaven" (7:12). Ezra would have ranked as the Secretary of State for Jewish affairs.

Ezra's journey required four months (7:9) because his party could not take the direct route across the desert from Babylon to Jerusalem. Instead, he traveled northwest and then southwest, about 900 miles.

Question 5. Refer back to Ezra 3:1-6. When talking about what we can sacrifice today, allow time for thoughtful reflection, and try to avoid glib answers.

Question 9. This question may stir up some differences of opinion. Guard the time and avoid tangents. Ask for specific things that have been done, to keep the discussion from being theoretical.

Question 12. List as many things as you can. Each quality should have some reasons to be included.

Study 5/The Journey Completed

Question 2. The missing Levites were essential, because the king had told Ezra to promote the law of Moses in Jerusalem. (See Numbers 1:47-54; 3:5-10 for more about the Levitical priests.) Thirty-eight Levites and twenty-two temple servants answered his call.

Question 4. Protection was critical because of wild beasts and robbers. They carried a huge amount of treasure (Ezra 8:25-27). Fasting was a sign of humility before God and prayer acknowledged dependence on God.

Question 7. Allow for discussion without acrimony, because Christians differ on these points. Perhaps someone would volunteer to tell a personal story about a special time of fasting and prayer.

Question 12. Keep the focus on leadership, noting that people can be spiritual leaders without having an official office or commission such as Ezra had.

Study 6/Sin Purged

Question 2. The culprits presumably were those who had been living in Judea all along, not those who had recently arrived. God had prohibited the Jews from marrying pagans (Exodus 34:12-15; Deuteronomy 7:1-4) because this would corrupt their faith. The chief example of this was the downfall of King Solomon (1 Kings 11:1-8).

Question 3. Tearing one's clothes was the usual sign of sorrow. Plucking out one's hair was highly unusual. Ezra sat down in the temple at the time of the evening sacrifice. As the Jews came to pray, they noticed his sadness. Then he began to pray aloud.

Question 4. This is one of the most moving prayers in the Bible. Although guiltless himself, Ezra identified with the sinners in his midst.

Question 7. This is perhaps the closest connection between Ezra and us. Take time to flesh out each part of his prayer and show how it applies to our prayer lives, public and private.

Question 8. These drastic measures of sending women and children away seem cruel and heartless. However, the survival of the Jewish faith was at stake.

Question 11. The list includes over 100 offenders. Perhaps these were among the prominent people. Many others were also implicated.

Question 13. Plan your time carefully to allow for a thorough review of Ezra the leader. Encourage people to think biblically about their own leadership roles (in whatever capacity) and the leaders they serve under in their churches.

Study 7/Nehemiah's Mission Launched

Nehemiah's Time Frame: The books of Ezra, Nehemiah, and Esther cover the last century of Jewish history in the Old Testament (circa 538–433 B.C.). Ezra and Nehemiah tell of three returns to Jerusalem. First, the main group returned with Zerubbabel in 538–537. Then eighty years later another party returned with Ezra in 458 B.C. Nehemiah and his entourage went back in 445. (For the destruction of Jerusalem and the captivity of the Jews in Babylon, read 2 Kings 24:18–25:30 and 2 Chronicles 36:11-21.) In the larger geopolitical scene, the Persians, led by Cyrus, defeated the Babylonian Empire in 539. The stories of Ezra and Nehemiah occurred during the reigns of five Persian kings, Cyrus, Cambyses, Darius I, Xerxes I, and Artaxerxes I (464–423 B.C.).

Question 2. In ancient kingdoms cupbearers were expected to be eminently trustworthy because they tasted and served the king's food and drink. Their role was critical because of the ever-present risks of poisoning by potential usurpers. Usually cupbearers were eunuchs. Jewish laws prohibited emascula-tion, but of course those laws meant nothing to the Persians. Susa was the winter capital of the Persian Empire. Consult a Bible-lands map to see its location relative to Jerusalem.

Question 3. The temple foundation had been laid and worship reinstated in Jerusalem. However, the city wall had not been rebuilt, leaving the Israelites vulnerable.

Question 5. Encourage the group to identify these elements quickly so as not to take too much time. Nehemiah shows here that he knew well God's promise in Deuteronomy 30:1-5. The phrase in Nehemiah 1:11, "in the presence of this man," refers to the Persian king. The *Good News Bible* version reads, "Give me success today and make the emperor merciful to me."

Question 7. The king asked Nehemiah how long he would be gone (Nehemiah 2:6). He returned twelve years later (Nehemiah 5:14), but he probably told the king he would be back sooner than that.

Question 9. Jerusalem's condition could be blamed on the decree of Artaxerxes that rebuilding cease (Ezra 4:7-23). Therefore, Nehemiah took great risks in proposing to rebuild a city whose chief reputation was the seat of rebellion. So we can understand why he made a secret inspection of the city and did not tell anyone what he was up to.

Question 10. Sanballat, Tobiah, and Geshem (see Nehemiah 4:1-9; 6:1-18; 13:4-9). Sanballat was governor of Samaria. Tobiah was his subordinate. Geshem ruled over Edom to the south.

Study 8/Persisting Despite Opposition

Question 3. Nehemiah was able to marshal virtually the entire community: priests, Levites, temple servants, goldsmiths, perfume makers, merchants, men and women, rulers and regular citizens. Some people were inspired to work on double sections. Knowing human nature very well, Nehemiah put people to work on sections near their own homes. Some noblemen, however, refused to work (Nehemiah 3:5).

Apparently while he was inspecting the walls (Nehemiah 2:11-17), Nehemiah made careful notes and rather detailed plans. The text does not say so specifically, but it is safe to assume that he assigned the various groups of workers to specific gates and sections of the wall.

Question 4. Work projects abound from volunteering in our communities to serving the church around the world.

Encourage people to give specific, concise ideas, so as not to eat up too much of your discussion time. Bring some projects from your church's missions committee for ideas.

Question 5. Much more was at stake here than the repairs. These leaders saw their political power melting away, together with their taxes. It was true that the walls were a complete shambles (Nehemiah 4:2). The walls had been burned, and the intense heat had disintegrated the local limestone.

Question 6. The seriousness of the threat posed by Sanballat and Tobiah is clearly revealed in the nature of Nehemiah's prayer requests. This prayer was not motivated so much by personal vengeance as it was by a concern for God's people and the honor of his name. For New Testament teaching on how to respond to provocations, see Romans 12:17-21 and 1 Peter 2:18-25.

Question 8. Encourage members to talk about how to integrate faith and hard work. Some would say prayer is the only right thing to do, while others tend to neglect prayer as a waste of time, preferring to attack problems without it.

Question 10. This discussion should offer hope and guidance to those who find it hard to balance spiritual priorities with trusting in human resources, strengths, and cleverness.

Question 11. Rich Jews took advantage of the plight of poor Jews by lending them money at exorbitant interest rates. Usury (Nehemiah 5:7) was prohibited by the laws of Moses (Exodus 22:25; Deuteronomy 23:20).

Question 12. Nehemiah had redeemed Jewish slaves. The nobles, knowing this, sold debt-ridden Jews into slavery. This dishonored God (Nehemiah 5:9). To seal his agreement with them and to warn them against going back on their word, he performed a symbolic act (Nehemiah 5:13). Instead of behaving like previous governors, who had gotten rich through salaries and taxes, Nehemiah set the example of compassion for the poor. He not only worked on the gates and walls but also refrained from buying cheap land (5:16). He provided food for the returning exiles (5:17) and hosted a great feast at his own expense (5:18).

Study 9/Reaching the Goal

Question 2. The plain of Ono (Nehemiah 6:2) was about twenty miles northwest of Jerusalem.

Question 3. Nehemiah smelled a rat. The invitation concealed a plot against his life.

Question 4. Our best principles are drawn from Christ's temptation by Satan. Jesus refused every offer. He knew his mission and calling, and he knew Scripture. The apostle Paul made clear the demarcation between believers and the forces of darkness (2 Corinthians 6:14-16). See also 1 John 2:15-17; 4:1-3; 5:21.

Question 5. Sanballet's letter was unsealed (Nehemiah 6:5) so that all who handled it could read it and spread the rumor about Nehemiah's revolt.

Question 7. Shemaiah (Nehemiah 6:10) was a false prophet who was bribed by Sanballet and Tobiah. "Shut in at his home" probably means he was in a state of prophetic ecstasy.

The facts in Nehemiah 6:17-19 show that there were traitors in Jerusalem who kept in touch with Tobiah. Treason was also involved in the marriages of Tobiah and Shecaniah's daughter, and Tobiah's son and Meshullam's daughter. Meshullam was at the same time building the walls (Nehemiah 3:4, 30).

Question 8. Only priests were allowed in the holy place of the temple (Nehemiah 6:10-11). If Nehemiah violated this provision, he would be discredited by the Jews.

Question 11. Nehemiah knew that if people were to move into Jerusalem, which is what he desired, they would need some assurance of protection for their safety.

Question 12. This is virtually the same list we saw in Ezra 2. It refers to the first and main party of Jews that departed Babylon for Jerusalem in 538 B.C.

Study 10/ God's Law Rediscovered

Question 2. Give ample time for listing all the details. Make this as colorful and dramatic as possible. Be sure to get the order of events straight: the first day of the month (Nehemiah 8:2) and the second day (8:13). This gathering was only a few days after the completion of the walls and gates, back on the twenty-fifth day of the sixth month (6:15).

We see Ezra here again. Since the king had commissioned him to teach God's laws (Ezra 7:25), he must have done this prior to Nehemiah's arrival. Few people had scrolls of their own, so they had to learn the law from public reading and teaching. But during the work on the wall, this was probably not possible.

Question 3. The leaders had a special interest in the law. They went to Ezra for private teaching and discovered the regulations for the Feast of Booths (Nehemiah 8:13-15).

Question 6. The Feast of Booths (8:13-18) is described in Leviticus 23:33-43, where it is called the Feast of Tabernacles. It commemorated God's care over the Jews on their forty-year journey through the wilderness en route from Egypt to Canaan.

Although there are no exact carryovers from the Feast of Booths, it is valuable to talk about ways Christians today can mark special occasions. Ask for specific examples people have seen and for celebrations or rituals they wish they would see.

Question 9. There is a difference in translations, some texts saying that Ezra made this prayer. Perhaps the Levites gave the prayer in Ezra's name.

Question 12. Be sure that people understand the meaning of confession. It is essential for their ongoing spiritual health and growth. Some may talk about making confessions to their priests. Try to avoid debate on this subject.

Question 13. This question may be difficult for some. Emphasize the importance of knowing the gospel facts about Jesus. Some may keep journals of their spiritual milestones, even on a daily basis. It's important for adults to be able to rehearse the basics of their own faith walk, including their failures, for the instruction and encouragement of children and youths.

Study 11/Convenant Confirmed

Question 4. Two major themes emerge in this document: (1) separation from surrounding pagans, and (2) extensive offerings.

Question 5. The Jews of Nehemiah's time were required by law to bring their offerings to the temple. For us, obedience to Christ and his church is not a matter of laws or legalism. Nevertheless, it is important to stress the practical implications of New Testament principles, a major one being that because of God's grace in Christ, we owe everything to him (Romans 12:1-2). We are not our own (2 Corinthians 5:15). Although we do not have a list of offerings like God gave the Jews, he expects us to work out a sacrificial lifestyle.

Question 8. Purification was accomplished by the sprinkling of people, priests, Levites, gates, and walls with the blood of sacrificial animals. This was done according to the laws of Moses.

Question 9. Our sin is an offense to God and has terrible effects in our lives. Only the blood of Jesus can make us clean from sin to worship God. See Romans 3:23; 6:23; Ephesians 2:8-9; Hebrews 9:22, 26; 10:11-14; 1 John 1:9.

Question 12. Considering Israel's abysmal record in the past, this was an outstanding achievement. It shows that Nehemiah not only knew how to build the walls but also to see that God's ancient requirements were met.

Study 12/Living Up to the Call

Note: Rather than discuss each of Nehemiah's reforms separately, look at the chapter as a whole and grasp the major themes and applications as they are developed in the flow of questions. This should be a significant wrap-up of what people have learned and what they want to do.

Question 2. In 433 B.C. Nehemiah left Jerusalem and returned to King Artaxerxes (verses 6-7), but when he came back to Jerusalem he found that the people had allowed various sins to creep into their social and religious life. Once again he asserted vigorous leadership (he was the governor) to clean up these abuses.

Question 4. These may not seem like big deals to us, but they were critical for the city's future spiritual welfare. The exiles had to be reminded that for such abuses their forefathers had been judged by God and banished to exile in Babylon. The high priest had given one of Jerusalem's enemies, Tobiah, quarters in rooms attached to the temple (verses 1-9). Tobiah was an Ammonite. The people were not providing for the needs of the Levites (verses 10-13). The people were violating the laws regarding the Sabbath (verses 15-22). They had married foreign women (verses 23-27). The objection to foreign women was not based on race, but on their idolatry.

WHAT SHOULD WE STUDY NEXT?

To help your group answer that question, we've listed the Fisherman Guides by category so you can choose your next study.

TOPICAL STUDIES

Angels, Wright

Becoming Women of Purpose, Barton

Building Your House on the Lord, Brestin

The Creative Heart of God, Goring

Discipleship, Reapsome

Doing Justice, Showing Mercy, Wright

Encouraging Others, Johnson

The End Times, Rusten

Examining the Claims of Jesus, Brestin

Friendship, Brestin

The Fruit of the Spirit, Briscoe

Great Doctrines of the Bible, Board

Great Passages of the Bible, Plueddemann

Great Prayers of the Bible, Plueddemann

Growing Through Life's Challenges, Reapsome

Guidance & God's Will, Stark

Heart Renewal, Goring

Higher Ground, Brestin

Images of Redemption, Van Reken

Integrity, Engstrom & Larson

Lifestyle Priorities, White

Marriage, Stevens

Miracles, Castleman

One Body, One Spirit, Larsen

The Parables of Jesus, Hunt

Parenting with Purpose and Grace, Fryling

Prayer, Jones

The Prophets, Wright

Proverbs & Parables, Brestin

Satisfying Work, Stevens & Schoberg

Senior Saints, Reapsome

Sermon on the Mount, Hunt

Spiritual Gifts, Dockrey

Spiritual Hunger, Plueddemann

A Spiritual Legacy, Christensen

Spiritual Warfare, Moreau

The Ten Commandments, Briscoe

Ultimate Hope for Changing Times, Larsen

Who Is God? Seemuth

Who Is the Holy Spirit? Knuckles & Van Reken

Who Is Jesus? Van Reken

Wisdom for Today's Woman: Insights from Esther, Smith

Witnesses to All the World, Plueddemann

Women at Midlife, Miley

Worship, Sibley

BIBLE BOOK STUDIES

Genesis, Fromer & Keyes
Exodus, Larsen
Ezra and Nehemiah,
   Reapsome
Job, Klug
Psalms, Klug
Proverbs, Wright
Ecclesiastes, Board
Jeremiah, Reapsome
Jonah, Habakkuk, &
   Malachi, Fromer & Keyes
Matthew, Sibley
Mark, Christensen
Luke, Keyes
John, Kuniholm
Acts 1–12, Christensen
Paul (Acts 13–28), Christiansen
Romans, Reapsome
1 Corinthians, Hummel

Strengthened to Serve
   (2 Corinthians),
   Plueddemann
Galatians, Titus & Philemon,
   Kuniholm
Ephesians, Baylis
Philippians, Klug
Colossians, Shaw
Letters to the Thessalonians,
   Fromer & Keyes
Letters to Timothy, Fromer &
   Keyes
Hebrews, Hunt
James, Christensen
1 & 2 Peter, Jude, Brestin
How Should a Christian
   Live? (1, 2 & 3 John),
   Brestin
Revelation, Hunt

BIBLE CHARACTER STUDIES

Abraham, Reapsome
David: Man after God's Own
   Heart, Castleman
Elijah, Castleman
Great People of the Bible,
   Plueddemann
King David: Trusting God for
   a Lifetime, Castleman
Men Like Us, Heidebrecht &
   Scheuermann

Moses, Asimakoupoulos
Paul (Acts 13–28), Christensen
Women Like Us, Barton
Women Who Achieved for
   God, Christensen
Women Who Believed God,
   Christensen